THE ART OF
KISSING

ISBN: 0-9786649-1-4

CONTENTS

"Arrange it so that the girl is seated against the arm of the sofa."

THE ART OF KISSING

The dictionary says that a kiss is "a salute made by touching with the lips pressed closely together and suddenly parting them." From this it is quite obvious that, although a dictionary may know something about words, it knows nothing about kissing.

If we are to get the real meaning of the word kiss, instead of going to the old fogies who compile dictionaries, we should go to the poets who still have the hot blood of youth coursing in their veins. For instance, Coleridge called a kiss, "nectar breathing." Shakespeare says that a kiss is a "seal of love." Martial, that old Roman poet who had ample opportunity to do research work on the subject, says that a kiss was "the fragrance of balsam extracted from aromatic trees; the ripe odor yielded by the teeming saffron; the perfume of fruits mellowing in their winter buds; the flowery meadows in the summer; amber warmed by the hand of a girl; a bouquet of flowers that attracts the bees."

Yes, a kiss is all of these... and more.

Others have said that a kiss was: the balm of love; the first and last of joys; love's language; the seal of bliss; love's tribute; the melting sip; the nectar of Venus; the language of love.

Yes, a kiss is all of these... and more.

For a kiss can never be absolutely defined. Because each kiss is different from the one before and the one after. Just as no two people are alike, so are no two kisses alike. For it is people who make kisses. Real, live people pulsating with life and love and extreme happiness.

DIFFERENT KINDS OF KISSES

Of course, there are different kinds of kisses. For instance, there is the kiss that the devout person implants on the ring of the Pope. There is the maternal kiss of a mother on her child. There is the friendly kiss of two people who are meeting or are separating. There is the kiss that a king exacts from his conquered subjects. But although all of these are called kisses, they are not the kisses that we are going to concern ourselves with in this book. Our kisses are going to be the only kind of kisses worth considering... the kisses of love. The kiss, perhaps, that Robert Bums had in mind when he wrote:

> *Honeyed seal of soft affections,*
> *Tenderest pledge of future bliss,*
> *Dearest tie of young connections,*
> *Love's first snowdrop, virgin kiss.*

The amazing thing about the kiss is that, although mankind has been kissing ever since Adam first turned over on his side and saw Eve lying next to him, there has been practically nothing written on the subject. Every year, hundreds of books are published telling you how to reduce, how to gain, how to get a job, how to cook, how to write and even how to live. But, on the art of kissing, very little has been written. One reason for this lack of proper instruction is accounted for by the Victorian sense of morals which has persisted through the ages. To the blue-nosed Puritans of the past, anything that concerned love was dirty, pornographical. John Bunyan's writings show what these Puritans thought of the kiss. He wrote in his infamous "The Pilgrim's Progress," "the common salutations of women I abhor. It is odious to me in whomsoever I see it. When I have seen good men salute those women that they have visited, or that have visited them, I have made my objections against it; and when they have answered that it was but a piece of civility, I have told them that it was not a comely sight. Some, indeed, have urged the holy kiss; but then, I have asked them why they make their balks; why they did salute the most handsome and let the ill-favored ones go." Perhaps old Bunyan thought that way because he was one of the "ill-favored" who went unkissed and were let "go."

But, nowadays, people have taken a broader outlook on life. Our plays are becoming more civilized and less stiff. Our arts are no more censored by laws. Our books are being written about subjects that no self-respecting author would ever have dared to put into a book. Birth-control, divorce and the science of marriage are common subjects for books. Even the strange vices of mankind are brought out into the open and discussed and not allowed to fester in the dark chambers of censorship. Yes, books like Vande Velde's "Ideal Marriage" and Slope's "Married Love" are openly sold in bookstores. But, nowhere, do we find a book which instructs people in the art of kissing, an art which is an absolute essential to a happy life, as we shall discuss in the oncoming pages of this book. Is it because we are not absolutely freed from the shackles of prudishness? In certain parts of this country, men have been arrested lor kissing their wives on the street! Is this civilization?

So it is, that this book is being written. It is going to be a manual of the kiss. In it we are going to discuss the most approved methods of kissing, the advantages of certain kinds and, with the disadvantages of others, the mental and physical reactions of kissers, historical episodes of kissing together with examples from the literature of the world in which kisses were the subject. So, gird up your loins, pucker up your lips and let's to the kissing arena!

WHY PEOPLE KISS

What happens when a man and a woman kiss?

That is to say, what happens to the various parts of the body when two people in love join their lips in bliss? Years ago, before our biologists knew of the existence of the glands in our bodies, one writer quoted a scientist as saying that "kissing is pleasant because the teeth, jawbones and lips are full of nerves, and when the lips meet an electric current is generated."

What nonsense! what utter nonsense!

In the first place, two people kiss because they are satisfying a hunger within them, a hunger that is as natural as the hunger for food, water and knowledge. It is the hunger of sex that drives them to each other. After that hunger has been satiated, then comes the hunger for a home, for children and for marital happiness. This hunger is instinctive, that is, we are born with it, all of us, and we cannot learn it or acquire it in any way.

WHY KISSING IS PLEASANT

Once this hunger for the opposite sex evidences itself, there occurs in the human body what is known as tumescence which, in simple language, is the rhythmical contraction of the various muscles of the body together with the functioning of certain glands, just which glands science has been unable to say definitely. Gland specialists know, by performing certain operations, that the adrenal, the pituitary, the gonad and certain other glands, control the sexual behavior of human beings. It is these glands that react, that secrete what are known as hormones into the blood which, in turn, carries them into the various organs effected by a sexual reaction.

Therefore, it can be seen that it is the partial satisfying of the sex-hunger that makes kissing pleasurable. Electricity is used for turning motors and lighting lamps and heating curling irons. But electricity does not give complete satisfaction to the kiss.

But enough of dry science!

We have ahead of us pleasurable reading of the bliss of the kiss. Now that we have learned why it is that men and women kiss, let us go into the methods used in kissing so as to derive the most satisfaction from this most soul-appeasing of pleasures.

APPROVED METHODS OF KISSING

The only kiss that counts is the one exchanged by two people who are in love with each other. That is the first essential of the satisfying kiss. For a kiss is really the union of two soul-mates who have come together because they were made for each other. The reason for this is that the kiss is really the introduction to love, true love. The kiss prepares the participants for the love life of the future. It is the foundation, the starting point of sexual love. And it is for that reason that the manner in which the kiss is performed is so vitally important.

There are still young women extant who believe that babies are the result of kisses! Actually this is a fact! And this condition exists because our parents, in the main, are either ignorant of the methods of explaining sex to their children or are too embarrassed to enlighten them. The result is that their children obtain their sexual information from the streets and alleys or else remain ignorant of it and believe such things as was mentioned above.

KISSES ARE BUT PRELUDES TO LOVE

Man and woman are born to love, marry and beget children. Woman is so physically constituted that she is the one who bears the child. Man, on the other hand, is given the duty of being the protector of his wife and, after they are born, of his children. Therefore, he must always be the one who takes the initiative. He must be strong, he must be willing, he must be physically able to take care of his charges. He must be the aggressor.

It is, therefore, necessary that the man be taller than the woman. The psychological reason for this is that he must always give the impression of being his woman's superior, both mentally and especially physically. The physical reason with which we are more concerned, is that if he is taller than his woman, he is better able to kiss her. He must be able to sweep her into his strong arms, and tower over her, and look down into her eyes, and cup her chin in his fingers and then, bend over her face and plant his eager, virile lips on her moist, slightly parted, inviting ones. All of this he must do with the vigor of an assertive male. And, all of these are impossible when the woman is the taller of the two. For when the situation is reversed, the kiss becomes only a ludicrous banality. The physical mastery is gone, the male prerogative is gone, everything is gone but the fact that two lips are touching two other lips. Nothing can be more disappointing.

PREPARING FOR THE KISS

A paragraph back, we mentioned that the woman's lips were slightly parted when she awaited the lips of her lover. There was a reason for using this description. Always, in any sort of kiss, just before the male's lips settle onto the lips of his partner, the female's lips should be slightly parted. One reason for this is that cherry-red lips serve as a charming frame for a row of gleaming, white, even teeth. The picture that confronts the kisser is one that draws him onward. And even, months later, when he thinks back to the kiss in the retrospect, he will remember that pretty little picture of the pearls of teeth nestling in their frame of cherries.

The deliciousness of a long-remembered kiss was beautifully expressed in a poem called, "Three Kisses," in which occurred the verse:

> *I gently raised her Sweet, pure face,*
> *Her eyes with radiant, love-light filled.*
> *That trembling kiss I'll ne'er forget*
> *Which both our hearts with rapture filled.*

Another reason for parting the lips is that there is a definite gratification the male obtains from the delicious odor that emanates from his loved one's mouth. John Secundus, in describing a kiss, said that his lover's kiss was like:

> *"...every aromatic breeze*
> *That wafts from Africa's spicy trees;"*

The odor of a woman's hair can send shivers of joy coursing up and down a man's spine. The odor of her body can convulse him with throes of passion. Odors are as necessary to love as is love itself. That is why it is so essential that the lips be parted just before the kiss. And that is why the breath should be kept always sweet and pure so that, when the lips are opened, the breath will be like an "aromatic breeze." Sometimes it is advisable to touch the corners of the mouth with perfume. But be certain that there is only the faintest suggestion of an odor and no more. Another thing, lipstick is definitely out in the kiss, because it comes off so readily. A very light coat of lipstick should be worn so that, when it does come off, it will not serve to betray you. Similarly, the teeth should be kept cleaned and polished. Nothing can dampen a young man's ardor, or a young woman's for that matter, than a row of brown-stained, unkept teeth.

HOW TO APPROACH A GIRL

In kissing a girl whose experience with osculation is limited, it is a good thing to work up to the kissing of the lips. Only an arrant fool seizes hold of such a girl, when they are comfortably seated on the sofa, and suddenly shoves his face into hers and smacks her lips. Naturally, the first thing he should do is to arrange it so that the girl is seated against the arm of the sofa while he is seated at her side. In this way, she cannot edge away from him when he becomes serious in his attentions. This done, on some pretext or another, such as a gallant attempt to adjust the cushions behind her, he manages to insinuate his arm, first around the back of the sofa and then, gradually, around her shoulders. If she flinches, don't worry. If she flinches and makes an outcry, don't worry. If she flinches, makes an outcry and tries to get up from the sofa, don't worry. Hold her, gently but firmly, and allay her fears with kind, reassuring words. Remember what Shakespeare said about "a woman's no!" However, if she flinches, makes an outcry, a loud, stentorian outcry, mind you, and starts to scratch your face, then start to worry or start to get yourself out of a bad situation. Such girls are not to be trifled with... or kissed. It is such as they, in most cases, who still believe the story of the stork which brings babies because of the consequences of a kiss.

But if your arm is comfortably reposed across the girl's shoulders and "all's right with the world," then your next step is to flatter her in some way. All women like to be flattered. They like to be told they are beautiful even when the mirror throws the lie back into their ugly faces.

Flatter her!

Catullus once wrote:

> *Kiss me softly and speak to me low;*
> *Trust me darling, the time is near,*
> *When we may live with never a fear*
> *Kiss me dear!*
> *Kiss me softly, and speak to me low!*

Tell her she is beautiful! Then, take a deep sniff of the perfume in her hair and comment on it. Tell her that the odor is like "heady wine." Tell her that her hair smells like a garden of roses. Tell her anything, but be sure to tell her something complimentary. This done, it is only a natural thing for you to do to desire to sink your nose deeper into her hair so that you can get the full benefit of its bouquet.

THE TECHNIQUE OF KISSING

Now is your chance! The moment you feel the tip of your nose touch her scalp, purse your lips and kiss her, the while you inhale a deep breath of air that is redolent with the exquisite odor of her hair. It is then but a few inches to her ear. Touch the rim of her ear with your lips in a sort of brushing motion. Breathe gently into the delicate shell. Some women react passionately to this subtle act. Brush past her here in this way again and note her reaction. If she draws her head away, return to her hair and sniff luxuriously of it. Then settle back to her ear, the while you murmur "sweet, airy nothings" into it. From the ear to her neck is but another few inches. Let your lips traverse this distance quickly and then dart into the nape and, with your lips well pursed, nip the skin there, using the same gentleness as would a cat lifting her precious kittens.

Then, with a series of little nips, bring your lips around from the nape of her neck to the curving, swerve of her jaw, close to the ear. Gently kiss the lobe of her ear. But be sure to return to the tender softness of her jaw. From then on, the way should be clear to you. Nuzzle your lips along the soft, downy expanse until you reach the corner of her lips. You will know when this happens because, suddenly, you will feel a strange stiffening of her shoulders under your arm. The reason for this is that the lips constitute one of the main erogenous zones of the body. The nerve ends in it are so sensitive that the slightest contact with them sends a pleasurable thrill immediately through the

"Take a deep sniff of the perfume in her hair and comment on it."

nervous system, through the medulla portion of the brain, back through the nervous system again, through branches which connect with motor nerves, in this case the nerves that control the sphincter muscles of the mouth and lips, and the sexual glands which were mentioned before.

In plain English, the kissee knows she is to be kissed.

Alright. You have subtly kissed the corner of her mouth. Don't hesitate. Push on further to more pleasurable spots. Ahead of you lies that which had been promised in your dreams, the tender, luscious lips of the girl you love. But don't sit idly by and watch them quivering.

Act!

Lift your lips away slightly, center them so that when you make contact there will be a perfect union. Notice, only momentarily, the picture of her teeth in her lips. And, then, like a seagull swooping gracefully down through the air, bring your lips down firmly onto the lips of the girl who is quivering in your arms.

Kiss her!

Kiss her as though, at that moment, nothing else exists in the world. Kiss her as though your entire life is wrapped up into the period of the kiss. Kiss her as though there is nothing else that you would rather be doing. Kiss her!

At this point, it is necessary for us to discuss a few subjects which are germane to the art of kissing, particularly in so far as they apply to what has just been described. For instance, there has been raised quite a fuss in regard to whether one should close one's eyes while kissing or while being kissed. Personally, I disagree with those who advise closed eyes. To me, there is an additional thrill in seeing, before my eyes, the drama of bliss and pleasure as it is played on the face of my beloved. I can see tiny wrinkles form at the corners of her eyes, wrinkles of joy. I can see fleeting spasms of happiness flit across her eyes. I can see these things and, in seeing them, my pleasurable reactions to the kiss are considerably heightened. In keeping my eyes open, I am giving pleasure not to one sense alone, the sense of touch, but to two senses, the senses of touch and of sight. These two, coupled with the sense of smell which is actuated by the perfume of her breath, all combine to make the kiss an exquisite, ineffable epitome of unalloyed bliss.

HOW TO KISS GIRLS WITH DIFFERENT SIZES OF MOUTHS

Another question which must be settled at this time concerns the size of the kissee's mouth. A consideration of this factor is important. Where the girl's mouth is of the tiny, rosebud type, then one need not worry about what to do. Merely follow the directions as they were outlined above. However, there are many girls whose lips are broad and generous, whose lips are on the order of Joan Crawford's, for instance. The technique in kissing such lips is different.

Different Sizes of Mouths Require a Different Technique in Kissing

For were one to allow his lips to remain centered, there would be wide expanses of lips, untouched and, therefore, wasted. In such cases, instead of remaining adhered to the center of the lips, the young man should lift up his lips a trifle and begin to travel around the girl's lips, stopping a number of times to drop a firm kiss in passing. When you have made a complete round of the lips, return immediately to the center bud and feast there. Feast there as did that lover of Fatimas, in Tennyson's poem, in which it was written that: "Once he drew, with one long kiss, my whole soul through my lips—as sunlight drinketh dew."

Then, sip of the honey. Like the bee that settles a flower, and sips in the nectar for honey, so should you sip in the nectar from between the lips of your love. And it is nectar. For there is in this mingling a symbol of the holy communion of the spirits of two soul-mates joined together in the bonds of an indissoluble love. It was a kiss such as this which caused the writer of an old German novel to write:

"Sophia returned my kiss and the earth went from under my feet; my soul was no longer in my body; I touched the stars; I knew the happiness of angels!"

ENJOY THE THRILLS OF KISSING

But don't be in a hurry! As in all matters pertaining to love, don't hurry the process of kissing. A kiss is too rapturous a thing to be enjoyed for the moment and the moment only. Linger longer on her lips than you have ever lingered before. Forget time. Forget everything but the kiss in which you are in the midst of. Don't be like that bashful young lover who, after a sweet, long kiss, drew his lips away from the lips of his charmer. Immediately, she burst out into tears.

"What's the matter?" he asked solicitously.

"You don't love me!" she said between sobs.

"But I do!"

"Then why did you draw your lips away?"

"I couldn't breathe," he said naively.

Breathe? Who wants to breathe, who even wants to think of breathing in the middle of an impassioned kiss? Breathe through your nose, if you have to breathe. But kiss, keep on kissing, as long as there is one minim of breath in you. Kiss, as Byron said we should kiss, with the "long, long kiss of youth and love!"

Recently, in Chicago, there was held a marathon kissing contest to determine which couple could hold their kiss the longest without being forced to separate. One pair was able to hold their kiss for fifteen hours. Think of that! Fifteen hours. And yet the naive lad stopped kissing because be couldn't breathe.

Elizabeth Barrett Browning must have spent many an ecstatic night of kissing with the poet, Robert Browning, if we are to judge from an excerpt from her "Aurora Leigh," in which she described a kiss as being "As long and silent as the ecstatic night."

Another poet, unknown, but certainly one who knew whereof he speaks, wrote the following poem which deserves to be quoted in its entirety.

> *Oh, that a joy so soon should waste,*
> *Or so sweet a bliss as a kiss*
> *Might not forever last!*
> *So sugared, so melting, so delicious.*
> *The dew that lies on roses,*
> *When the morn herself discloses,*
> *Is not so precious.*
> *Oh, rather than I would it smother*
> *Were I to taste such another.*

It should be my wishing
That I might die kissing.

At this point, it should be explained that the lips are not the only part of the mouth which should be joined in kissing. Every lover is a glutton. He wants everything that is part of his sweetheart, everything. He doesn't want to miss a single iota of her "million-pleasured joys" as Keats once wrote of them. That is why, when kissing, there should be as many contacts, bodily contacts, as is possible. Snuggle up closely together. Feel the warm touch of each other's bodies. Be so close that the rise and fall of each other's bosoms is felt by one another.

Get next to each other.

And, this same thing applies to the mouth in kissing. Don't be afraid to kiss with more than your lips. After your lips have been glued together for sometime, open them slightly. Then put the tip of your tongue out so that you can feel the smooth surface of your kissee's teeth. This will be a signal for her to respond in kind. If she is wholly in accord with you, if she is, truly, your real love-mate, then you will notice that she, too, has opened her

"Snuggle up closely together"

lips slightly and that, soon, her teeth will be parted. Then, if she is all that she should be, she should project the tip of her tongue so that it meets with the tip of yours.

Heaven will be in that union!

Lava will run through your veins instead of blood. Your breath will come in short gasps. There will rise up in you an overpowering, overwhelming surge of emotion such as you have never before experienced. If you are a man, you will clutch the shoulders of your loved one and sense a shudder course through you that makes you pant. If you are a woman, and being kissed, you will feel a strange languor passing through your limbs, your entire body. A shudder will go through you. You will moan in the delicious transports of love. And, in all probabilities, you will go faint because the blood in your veins will be rushing furiously into your entire system and away from your head. Thus, you will be unable to think any longer.

You will only be able to feel, to feel the most exquisite of pleasures that it has been your lot to feel.

THE FRENCH "SOUL" KISS

But don't stop at this.

Surely, there is more to your tongue than merely its tip. Probe further. Go deeper. Gently caress each other's tongues. For, in doing this, you are merging your souls. That is why this kiss was called the "soul" kiss by the French who were said to be the first people to have perfected it. The French have always been a liberal minded people. And, it is because of the fact that they dropped Puritanism many years ago, that they were able to perfect themselves in the art of love and, particularly, in the art of kissing.

Learn from the French.

Learn also from the old Romans, especially Catullus, whose love poems to Lesbia have lived through the ages because of the sincerity of his passion and the genius of his ability to express his emotions in the form of beautiful poetry. For it was Catullus who wrote:

> *"Then to those kisses add a hundred more,*
> *A thousand to that hundred, so kiss on!*
> *To make that thousand up to a million;*
> *Treble this million, and when that is done,*
> *Let's kiss afresh, as when we first begun."*

Kisses cost nothing. So kiss on. There is one thing that you cannot take away from people and that is the ability to make love to each other. Despite the fact that the world suffered from a long depression, people continued to get married and they continued to have children. In fact, according to recently released figures, there were more children born during the depression than there had been in good times. This means that, although married people did not have money, they still had themselves. They still had love. They still had the ability to kiss as they pleased and when they pleased and as often as they pleased.

Another poet asks:

> *What is a kiss? alack, at worst,*
> *A single drop to quench a thirst,*
> *Tho oft it proves in happier hour,*
> *The first sweet drop of one long shower.*

Because kisses cost nothing.

So kiss on. Keep on kissing. Rare old Ben Jonson realized this when he wrote that, if he had one wish, it would be that he could die kissing. But it is not only the robust and lusty poets, like Ben Jonson, who are gluttons for kisses. There has been attributed to John Ruskin, an old fogy of a philosopher if ever there was one, a request from him to a young lady friend of his that she "kiss him not sometimes but continually." Still another poet wrote:

> *Kisses told by hundreds o'er;*
> *Thousands told by thousands more.*
> *Millions, countless millions then*
> *Told by millions o'er again;*
> *Countless as the drops that glide*
> *In the ocean's billowy tide,*
> *Countless as yon orbs of light*
> *Spangled o'er the vault of night*
> *I'll with ceaseless love bestow*

> *On those cheeks of crimson glow,*
> *On those lips so gently swelling,*
> *On those eyes such fond tales telling.*

PUT VARIETY INTO YOUR KISSES

It is with the last few lines of this poem that our next subject for discussion concerns itself. As was mentioned before, the true lover is not satisfied with only one or two contacts. He wants nothing to be held from him. It is for that reason that, when kissing a girl, after you have given sufficient time to the kissing of her lips, you should vary your kissing by diverting your zeal to other portions of her face.

Robert Herrick, who wrote many beautiful love lyrics in his day, has a poem which ideally synthesizes this idea of varied kisses. In it he says:

> *It isn't creature born and bred*
> *Between the lips all cherry-red;*
> *It is an active flame that flies*
> *First to the babies of the eyes;*
> *Then to the cheek, the chin and ear;*
> *It frisks and flies—now here, now there—*
> *'Tis now far off, and then 'tis near;*
> *Here and there and everywhere.*

Let us say that you have revelled in a sweet, long kiss. Suddenly, you see your loved one's eyes close as though in a moment of weariness. Gently detach your lips from hers and raise them up to her closed eyelids. Drop a kisslet first on one eyelid and then on the other. Feel the rolling orb quiver under your lips. Then, when you have done this, run your lips down along the line of her nose, stopping at odd times to purse them into a tiny kiss. When you reach the wrinkle of her nostrils, bury your lips deeply into the curve and kiss little niblets into first one and then the other. If her eyes still are closed, repeat the process.

But return to the lips.

Never forget this important injunction, "Return to the lips," for they can never become satiated with love's ardent kisses. The little kisses that you have deposited on her eyes and her nose serve only to vary the menu of love. They are but spice to the main course of love's banquet which should always be the "lip kiss."

THE "VACUUM" KISS

This time, when your eager lips have been deposited on the eager lips of the girl, try to vary the kiss. For instance, instead of using the soul kiss, try what is known as the "vacuum kiss." Here you start off by first opening your mouth a trifle just after you have been resting peacefully with closed lips. Indicate to your partner, by brushing her teeth with the tip of your tongue, that you wish for her to do likewise. The moment she responds, instead of caressing her mouth, suck inward as though you were trying to draw out the innards of an orange. If she knows of this kiss variation, your maid will act in the same way and withdraw the air from your mouth. In this fashion, in a very short while, the air will have been entirely drawn out of your mouths. Your lips will adhere so tightly that there will almost be pain, instead of pleasure. But it will be the sort of pain that is highly pleasurable. That may sound odd but, nevertheless, it is a fact. Pain becomes so excruciating as to become pleasure. This subject will be gone into very shortly in regard to what is known as the "bite kiss." But, at present, let us continue with the "vacuum kiss."

This kiss must, of necessity, last a comparatively short time. There is too much strain on the delicate mouth tissues and the muscles tire very easily. It is for that reason that this kiss should be shortened. However, there is a special technique to be used to terminating it. When you decide that you have had enough of it, don't suddenly tear your mouth away. At least, don't do it if there are other people present in the house. For,

they will become startled by the sound of a loud report which will result if you act suddenly. Any vacuum when suddenly opened to air gives off a loud popping noise. The procedure is simply to open first a corner of your mouth. You will hear a faint hissing sound when this is done. Immediately, you will find the pressure in your mouth lessen.

The Vacuum Kiss

The muscles will relax. And a delicious sense of torpor will creep over your entire body, giving it a lassitude that is almost beatific.

But that is not all.

To every large dinner, there is always added a dessert or a lagniappe which is a topping-off tid-bit of the evening. The same should apply to the "vacuum kiss." The minute you release your lips, lift them away from the tired lips of your lover. Then, without wasting a minute's time, gently, delicately, softly, sensitively, oh so lightly, lower your pursed lips and place a tiny little kiss into the almost bruised lips of the girl. It is this little act of sympathy and condolence that makes the tie between you all the more firm. It tells the girl that you know how she feels and that you sympathize with her.

While resting from the joy-laden ardors of such a kiss, a few more variations are permissible and advisable. There should never be a let-down in a kissing session. Every moment must be filled with kisses. But they do not have to be kisses of the mouth. There are other kisses which, although they are not as satisfying as the lip kisses, still serve to keep the blood burning.

THE "SPIRITUAL" KISS

For instance, there can be kisses exchanged merely in intense glances. A sort of "spiritual kiss" can pass between the adoring eyes of a pair of lovers. The hot blooded Latin races know the power of such kisses. Their fiery temperaments are ever questing for new delights, for variations, for delightful and artful ways of adding to the pleasure of love. There is a poem extant written by a young Spanish poet to his sloe-eyed, raven-tressed senorita. No doubt it was sung by him under her balcony while the romantic moon streamed down liquid beams. But the poem quite amply describes this point of kissing with things other than your lips.

> *Then she kisses with her eyelids,*
> *Kisses with her arching eye-brows,*
> *With her soft cheek softly rubbing,*
> *With her chin and hands and fingers,*
> *All the frame of Manuela,*
> *All her blood and all her spirit,*
> *All melt down to burning kisses.*

There, perhaps fifteen feet away from him, was the light of her love. Yet, by means of her eyes, she was able to kiss him so that their love continued to flower.

THE EYELASH KISS

A variation of this eye kiss can be practiced as a tender diversion. After an intense period of "soul kissing" or vacuum kissing" has been indulged in and both lovers lie back tiredly, looking into each other's eyes, the young man should lean over the face of the girl. But, instead of implanting his lips on hers, he should bring his cheek into direct contact with her cheek again. Then, when this is done, he should lower his eyelash so that they enmesh with the eye-lash of his partner. This, of course, is done one eye at a time. And when the enmeshing process is complete, each should gently raise and lower his or her eyelids. The contact of the hair of the eyelash is one that is almost indescribable. Suffice it to say, it is a charming bypath in the meadows of love that is pleasant, provocative and yet not exhausting.

THE "PAIN" KISS

A while back, mention was made of the "pain kiss." It is with this seemingly paradoxical pleasure that we shall deal with now. First of all, it is necessary to explain that, although an act can be painful, it can still be pleasurable. The explanation is merely another indication of the variability of human nature. To begin, there are some people who derive an extreme pleasure out of being whipped or burned or beaten. There is no rational explanation for this strange delight. The fact remains that they react pleasurably to pain. These people are called masochists. Similarly, there are other people who derive the same pleasure out of being the ones who inflict the pain or perform the beating. Their abnormality, too, is inexplicable. They are called sadists.

The point is this: these people have these strange desires in extremes. But normal people have similar desires but they are not so strong. They are present only in minute degrees. That is why some of us deliberately uncover ourselves in cold weather or continue to pick at a sore tooth although the act pains us. It is for this reason that most of us are able to derive pleasure from the "pain kiss."

The "pain kiss" is simply a tiny bite, a love nip. Catullus, who knew his kissing, if we are to judge from the many poems he left on the subject, once wrote:

> *Whom wilt thou for thy lover choose?*
> *Whose shall they call thee, false one, whose?*
> *Who shall thy darted kisses sip,*
> *While thy keen love-bites scar his lip?*

THE "NIP" KISS

Horace, another Roman, whose kissing proclivities have come down through the ages because of his love poems, also wrote something about the "nip-kiss" when he said:

> *Or on thy lips, the fierce, fond boy*
> *Marks with his teeth the furious joy.*

So you see, it is perfectly normal people, if you can call poets normal people, who indulge in the "pain kiss" and derive intense pleasure from it. Punishment, after all, can be more than painful. For instance, in another poem, a poet says:

> *And if she dared her lips to pout,*
> *Like many pert young misses,*
> *I'd wind my arms her waist about*
> *And punish her with kisses.*

Naturally, in the "nip-kiss" the kisser is not supposed to open his mouth like the maw of a lion and then sink his fangs

into the delicate flesh of the kissee. Ridiculous! The procedure is the same as the ordinary kiss except that, instead of
closing your lips with the kiss, you leave them slightly open
and, as though you were going to nibble on a delicious tid-
bit, take a playful nip into either the nape of the neck, the
cheek or the lips. Just a nip is enough. And the resultant pleasure, I assure you, will more than compensate for the slight
inconvenience of pain.

Now there might be some of you who may wonder why
such kissing subterfuges and substitutes are necessary. It is
only that man is a questing animal. He is never satisfied with
the ordinary and commonplace because the commonplace,
after a time, becomes very boring. Not that I mean to infer
that the usual "lip-kiss" is commonplace. Absolutely not. The
"lip-kiss," as I have mentioned before, is the *piece de resis-
tance*, the main course in the "banquet of love" as the poet,
Ovid, called it. But imagine a meal in which there were seven
courses of filet mignon or seven courses of lobster. You'd get
sick and tired of a tender filet after the third course, wouldn't
you? And after the second lobster, you wouldn't be able to
look a lobster in the eye, that is, providing a lobster has eyes.
So you see why it is that if the lip-kiss were indulged in exclu-
sively, you would reach a point where it would lose all of its
rapturous savor.

VARIATION KISSES ARE THE SPICE OF LOVE

A variation of the "lip-kiss" can be performed very nicely.
Instead of pressing the lips together at one spot, start at one

corner of the mouth and brush your closed lips across the entire mouth. A variation of this, in turn, is to part your lips slightly and, with the tip of your tongue in the groove that separates the two lips, brush your lips from side to side. Naturally, additional variations to this last variation suggest themselves immediately to the aware practitioner of the kiss. In fact, to such a person, there should come up hundreds of other variations to titillate and titivate the senses.

One such variation suggests itself. Technically, it is not exactly a variation but simply a variation in the technique of the ordinary "lip-kiss." It employs the use of the "delayed action" in its execution. The old story of the fox and the grapes which were tantalizingly dangled over his head is the foundation for the method. Simply, the procedure is this: just before lowering your lips for the kiss, instead of planting the kiss, draw your head back again. Then, hold your lips in readiness but do not kiss. Hold this position for as long as possible, the while you smile tantalizingly into the eyes of the girl. Finally, when both you and she can stand the suspense no longer, then lower your lips, slowly, as slowly as you possibly can, and imprint the seal of love onto the avid mouth of your loved one. After that, the technique calls for no specific action. Kissing, like loving, is instinctive.

ELECTRIC KISSING PARTIES

Some few years ago, a very peculiar kissing custom arose which deserves mention here because, from it, we can learn how to adapt the method to our modern devices. At that time, when young people got together, they held, what was then known as, "electric kissing parties." Young people are ever on the outlook for novel ways of entertaining themselves. In fact, when ether was first developed as an anesthetic, the young bloods of the town used to form "ether-sniffing" parties in which they got a perfectly squiffy ether "jag." But to return to the "electric kisses." An excerpt from a contemporary writer will, perhaps, give us some idea of what happened.

"The ladies and gentlemen range themselves about the room. In leap year the ladies select a partner, and together they shuffle about on the carpet until they are charged with electricity, the lights in the room having been first turned low. Then they kiss in the dark, and make the sparks fly for the amusement of the onlookers."

The same sort of experiment could be performed nowadays, on cold, dry nights when the air is overloaded with electricity. But be certain that neither you nor your partner touches each other after shuffling furiously on the carpet with your feet. Merely lean over slowly and, when your lips are about half an inch apart, slow the process down even more until the spark jumps. However, considerable practice should be had before this kiss variation can be done successfully. The natural reaction to this sort of shock is to pull away from each other. But, try to resist this natural impulse because, if you do not kiss the moment after the shock has been perpetrated, the pleasure will be all gone.

Once you have practiced this for some time, you will become so inured to the slight shock that you will seek more potent electric shocks. These can be obtained with the use of an electric vibrator or, in fact, any device that is worked from a battery and a coil which steps up the weak 3 volts of the battery. Shooting galleries have electricity testing devices of this nature which have two handles. No matter what you use, the method is as following: first you take hold of one pole of the live wire, of the handle of the machine, if that is what you are using. Then, your partner should take hold of the other pole, or handle. This done, bring your lips together until, there is about an eighth of an inch separating your lips. At this moment, turn the rheostat that increases the current. As soon as the charge is strong enough, a sudden, intense spark will jump the gap of your lips. Again, learn not to flinch but to seize hold of the opportunity of bringing your lips together in a grand, climactic kiss. The advantage of this method is that you can regulate the electrical charges so that, when you become inured to one strength, you can increase the current almost indefinitely.

A word of warning, however, is apropos here. Be satisfied with the current generated by this battery set. Don't be like a young friend of mine who discovered that the battery set, even at its highest output, was too weak for him and his partner. Being of an experimental nature, he decided to see what would happen were he to use the ordinary house current as the electrical stimulus. And so, together with his partner, he placed himself in front of an electric wall outlet into which he had screwed a plug and a wire whose end had been frayed so that the two wires were separated. Taking hold of one wire, he advised the girl to take hold of the other. Then, using the usual "electric-kiss" technique, he bent over and started to bring his lips slowly towards the girl's lips. He got as far as about half an inch from her lips, and that's all. Because, a moment later, be saw a blinding flame sear across his eyes and he felt an enormous blow jolt him off his feet. When he came to enough to realize where he was, he found himself asprawl on the floor, his girl friend in a similar position a few feet away. The result was a pair of burned lips and a combined determination to stick to the old fashioned way of kissing. The burned lip will always spurn the flame.

THE DANCING KISS

A very pleasant way to kiss is found in the "dancing kiss." Here, again, it is the closeness of the bodies of the participants that adds to the enjoyment. What more could a pair of lovers ask for than a dimly lighted dance floor, the tender, rhythmical strains of a waltz being played by Wayne King, their arms around each other, their eager young bodies kissing each other in a myriad of excitable places, the while, their cheeks meet in glowing, velvety strokes? Naturally, in such situations, the rules of social etiquette will not allow the pair to enjoy an extremely appropriate "lip kiss." Although this can very easily be accomplished in the privacy of one's parlor while the radio is broadcasting the music. In fact, the "electric kiss" can be ideally performed under these circumstances. But, when dancing in a public place, the only kisses allowed would be those surreptitious ones stolen under the straying eye of the chaperone. Under the pretense of whispering pretty nothings into your partner's shell of an ear, allow your lips to touch her earlobe, her cheek and her chin. A few covert eye kisses, perhaps, can be stolen in this manner, too. But, these stolen sweets should suffice the happy couple until they return home. Then, stimulated by the forepleasure of these previous non-lip kisses, the pair can indulge in all the variations listed in this booklet, to their hearts' and their lips'

The Dancing Kiss

content. The while they recall, perhaps, those lines from Sir John Suckling's "Ballad of a Wedding," which went:

> *Oh, they sudden up and rise and dance;*
> *Then sit again, and sigh, and glance;*
> *Then dance again, and kiss.*

THE SURPRISE KISS

A most charming manner of kissing is called the "surprise kiss." This is performed when one of the parties has fallen asleep, on the sofa, let us say. On entering the room, when the other sees his lover asleep, he should tip-toe softly over to her. Then, lowering his head slowly, he should implant a soft, downy, feathery kiss squarely on her lips. This first kiss should be a very light one. But, thereafter, the intensity of the kisses should increase until the sleeping one has awakened and, of course, even beyond that. The effect of such an awakening to a sleeper is almost heavenly. For, while in the midst of a dream, a pleasant one, most likely, for it will concern the other half of the couple, she feels vaguely, faintly, as though it were the touch of a butterfly's wing, a subtle kiss on her lips. Naturally, in the depths of her sleep, she imagines that it is part of her dream and the result is a pleasant sensation, indeed. Then, gradually, although still asleep, she feels the kisses continue. And the pleasantness continues. Then, as she starts to come out of her sleep, she realizes that the kisses are too real for a dream. But she is sure that she is dreaming. And so, immediately, a relapse from the happiness sets in and a twinge of sadness comes over her because she knows that, instead of being with her lover, she is only dreaming of him. Imagine, then, her extreme gratification, when, while thinking these drab thoughts, she feels the actuality of an intense, ardent kiss on her lips. Her heart flutters wildly. Her pulse runs riot. Perhaps she is not asleep, she argues to herself. Then she opens her eyes. And she sees the darling face of her beloved bending over her. And she feels the sensuous touch of his lips on hers. Truly, no awakening can be more pleasurable!

KISSING UNDER THE MISTLETOE

Perhaps, in conclusion, it would be appropriate to make mention of a few kissing customs which have intrigued mankind. For instance, there is the rite of kissing under the mistletoe at Christmas time. The origin of this custom is uncertain. Suffice it to say, it must have been started by some woman because, in it, the rule is that if a woman is caught standing under a sprig of mistletoe, any man has the right to kiss her, peremptorily, without asking her permission or begging her pardon. Here is one time when social convention closes its eyes to lover's delights. For, then, you can seize hold of the girl with impunity and smack her to your heart's content without being socially ostracized for it.

KISSING GAMES

One wonders at the prevalence of kissing games in this civilization. Games on the order of "Post Office," "Kiss the Pillow" and innumerable others which have been devised for the jovial disports of lovers. In these games, because they are games, it is perfectly legitimate for two people to kiss. In fact, in the game "Post Office" this kissing is encouraged behind closed doors where the happy couple are alone in a room. The game is so widespread that comment in regard to the manner in which it is played would be extraneous here. But, what would make an excellent topping off for this booklet, would be a conjecture as to the reason for the prevalence of such games, even during the dreaded Victorian times, when etiquette was so strict that the dictum was made forbidding the placing of a book by a female author next to a book written by a man!

These kissing games existed and shall continue to exist because man and woman must kiss. In fact, man is the only animal who uses the kiss to express his love and affection. Dogs, cats and bears lick their offspring. Horses and cows rub noses and necks. Birds nestle together.

But only mankind kisses.

Only mankind has the reason, the logic, the happy faculty of being able to appreciate the charm, the beauty, the extreme pleasure, the joy, the passionate fulfillment of the kiss! Nature kisses, in her way, but nature hasn't the brains to profit from the kiss. Only man can do this.

Perhaps it would be appropriate to conclude this summary of the art of kissing with an excerpt from Shelley's immortal poem in which occur the following lines;

> *See the mountains kiss high heaven,*
> *And the waves clasp one another.*
> *No sister flower would be forgiven*
> *If it disdained its brother.*
>
> *And the sunlight clasps the earth,*
> *And the moonbeams kiss the sea;*
> *What are all these kissings worth*
> *If thou kiss not me?*

NOTES

NOTES

NOTES

NOTES